Coloring Book

ANIMALS
of
ASIA

Mark Shawe

Book Series: Animal Planet

In this Coloring Book you will find:

- 20 original realistic full-page images of wild animals of Asia on single-sided sheets to prevent bleed-through
- 60 interesting unusual facts about the animals

Grab you favorite tool: pencils, crayons, markers or paints, and start coloring!

ISBN: 9781079224740

WORLD MAP

Camel

You've probably heard that camels store water in their humps. But, in fact, humps are fat storages! Camels store away some food to sustain them in the deserts. These amazing animals can survive 5 days without water when the temperature rises above 90' F, and for 6-7 months in winter time. They can burp the food back into their mouths and chew it again, just like cows!

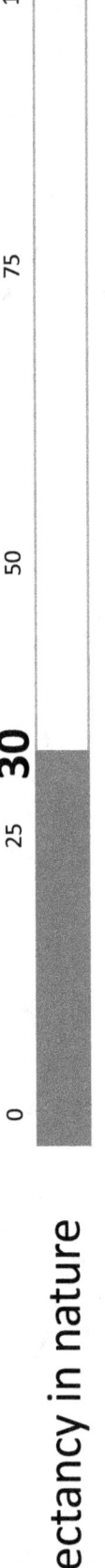

life expectancy in nature

weigh up to   1000 kg (2200 lb)

| 0 | 25 | **30** | 50 | 75 | 100 |

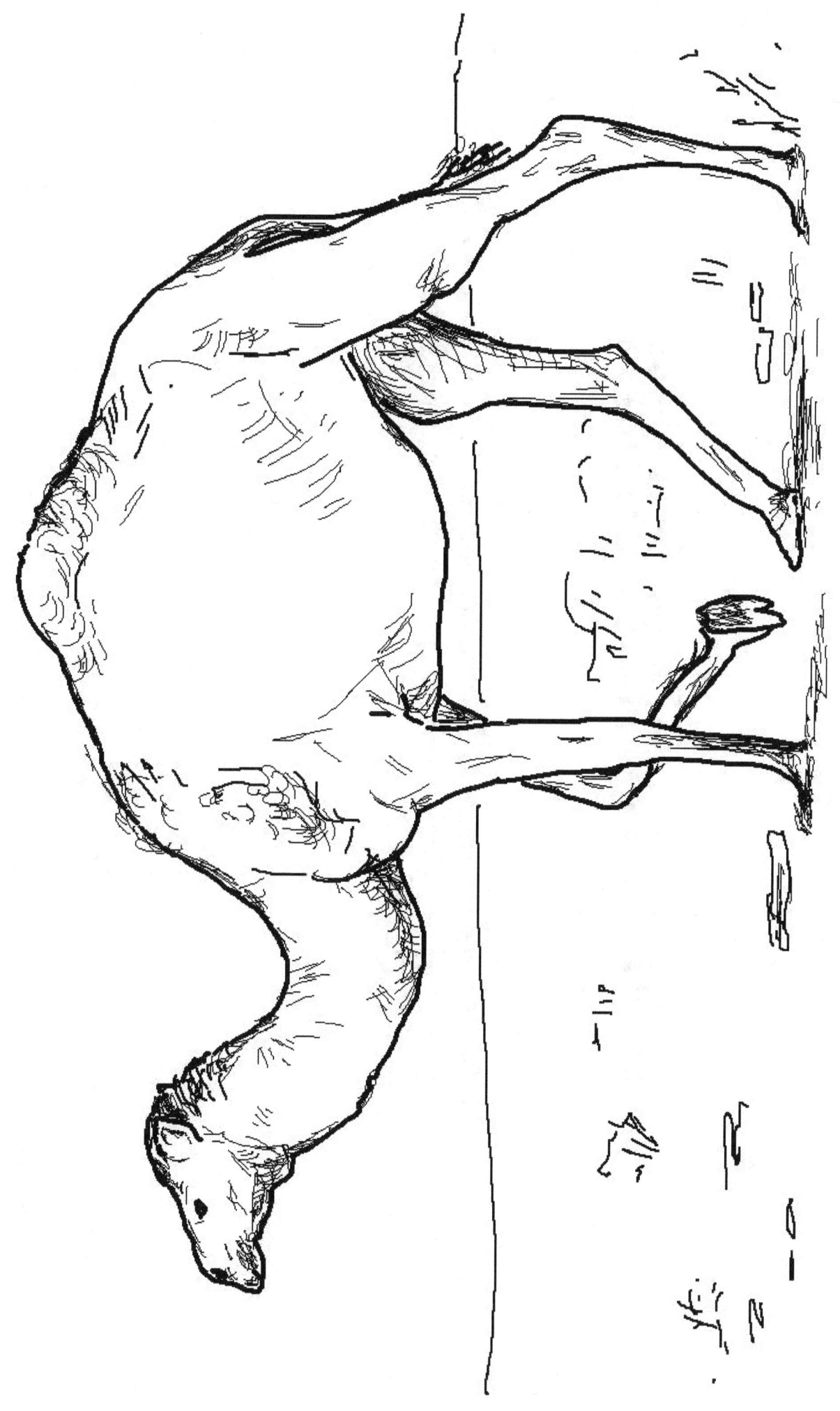

Gaur, Indian bison

There's no better way to describe these creatures – cows on steroids. They are heavy, large, stout and muscular. They don't make good pets – way too wild.

life expectancy in nature

0   25 **30**   50   75   100

weigh up to   1500 kg (3305 lb)

Asian elephant

Indian elephants are large, herbivorous mammals, which means that they eat plants, not animals. Their immense size means they are often classified as one of the "mega-fauna" animals. Elephant herds have "aunties" who look after the babies of other females – free baby-sitters!

life expectancy in nature

weigh up to 5500 kg (12125 lb)

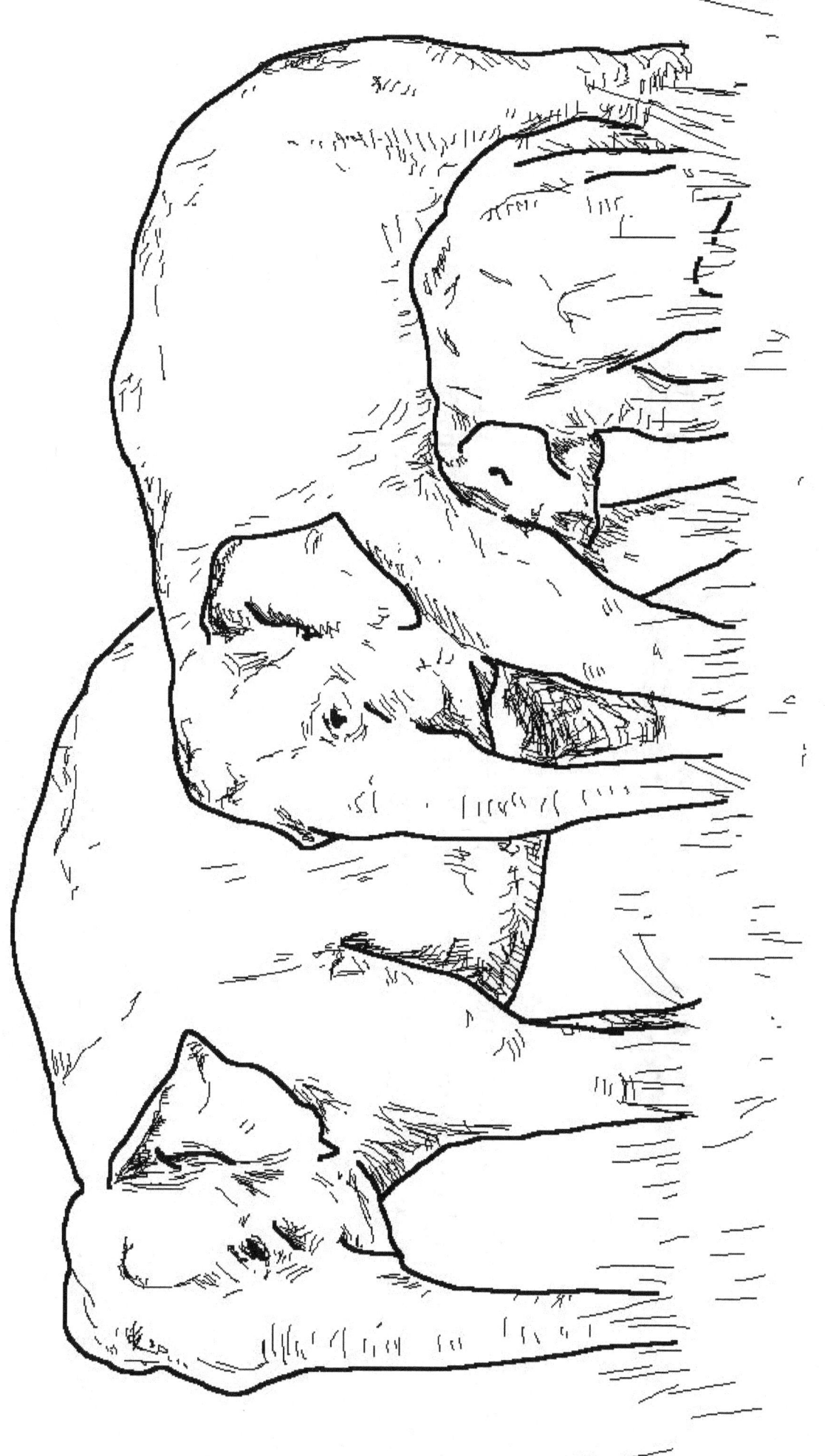

Asiatic black bear

This bear has a noticeable white necklace as if he is wearing a knight's pendant. Asiatic black bears are the most bipedal of all bears, and have been known to walk upright for over a quarter mile!

life expectancy in nature

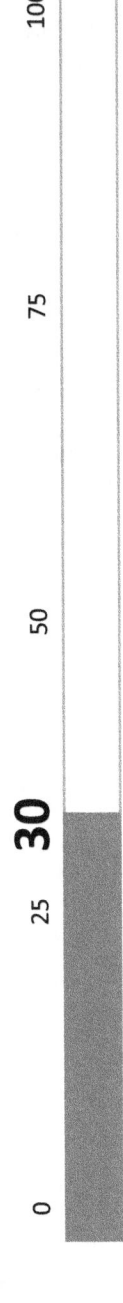

0   25   **30**   50   75   100

weigh up to   600 kg (1300 lb)

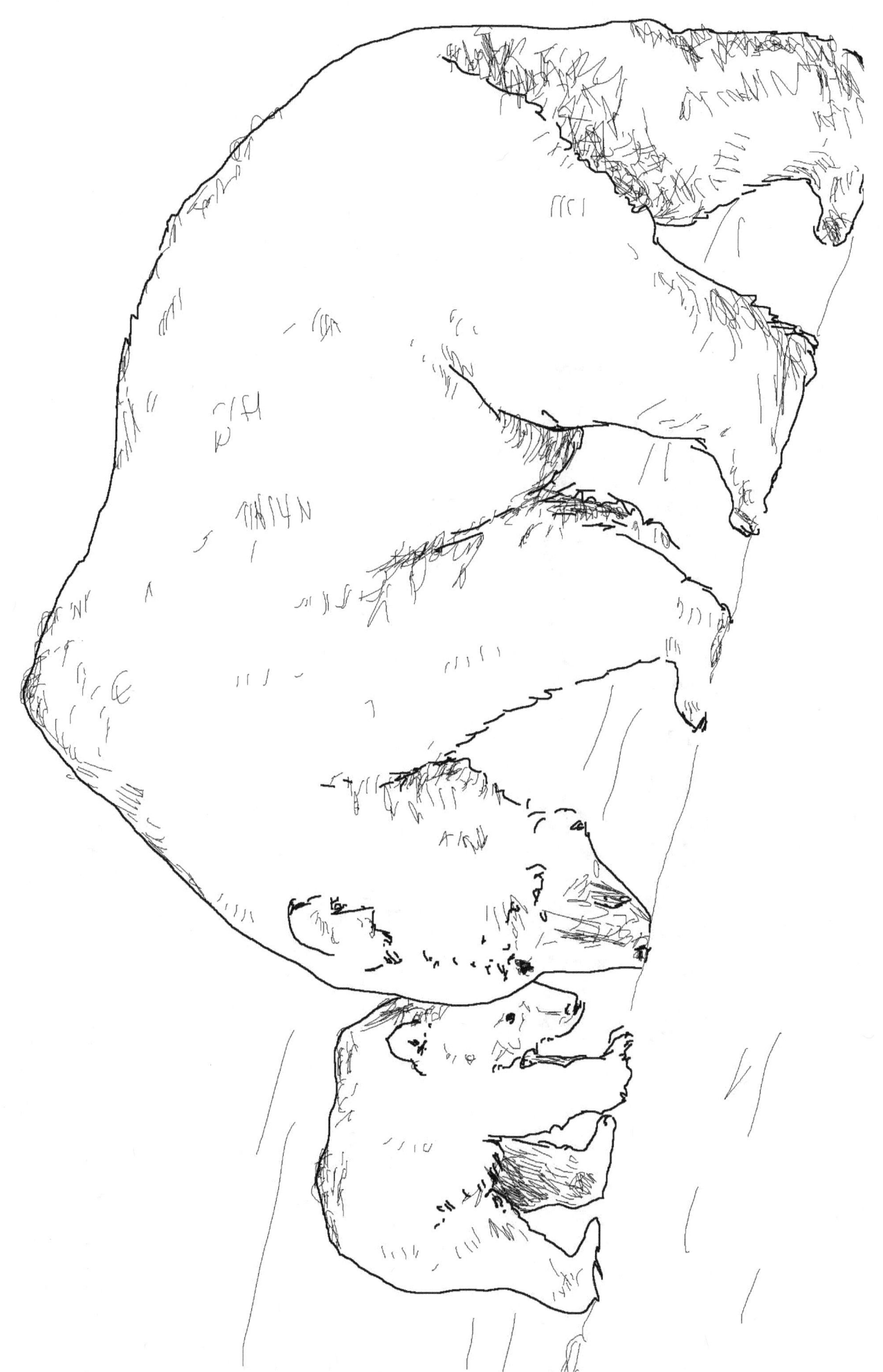

Asiatic wild dog - Dhole - Red wolf

A curious combination of a dog, a wolf, a jackal and a fox is found in this animal. They let the pups feed first. Their dens vary from simple earth holes to complex multilevel structures with multiple entrances, sharp turns and caverns.

life expectancy in nature

| 0 | **8** | 25 | 50 | 75 | 100 |

weigh up to   17 kg (38 lb)

Orangutan

Orangutans are the only great apes species with a native habitat outside of Africa. The word orangutan comes from the Malay language and means 'person of the forest' – from the words 'orang' meaning people and 'hutan' meaning forest. Orangutans are very inventive – they use leafy branches to shelter themselves from rain and sun. When it rains very hard the orangutan makes an umbrella for himself out of big leaves.

life expectancy in nature

0   25   **30**   50   75   100

weigh up to   90 kg (196 lb)

Japanese crane

The Japanese crane, also known as the red-crowned crane is sacred and seen as a symbol of fidelity, good luck, love and long life in the Orient. They mate for life and like other cranes, are well known for their wonderful dances that bond the couples. Shortly after the end of World War II, the folded origami cranes came to symbolize a hope for peace through Sadako Sasaki and her unforgettable story of perseverance.

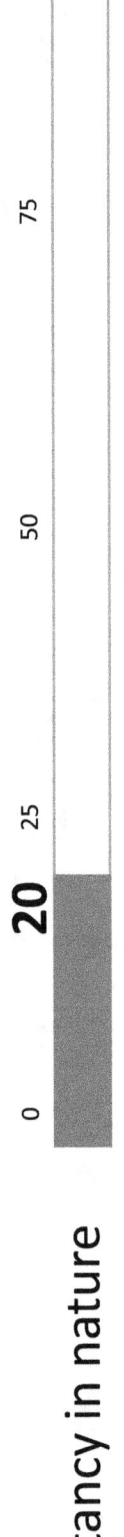

life expectancy in nature

0   **20**   25   50   75   100

weigh up to   7 kg (15,5 lb)

Amur pike

The pike is one of the most easily recognized fish in the world, mainly due to their elongated body shape and sharply pointed head. The teeth of the pike are one of its most characteristic features as they are pointed and very sharp, to make catching prey more efficient.

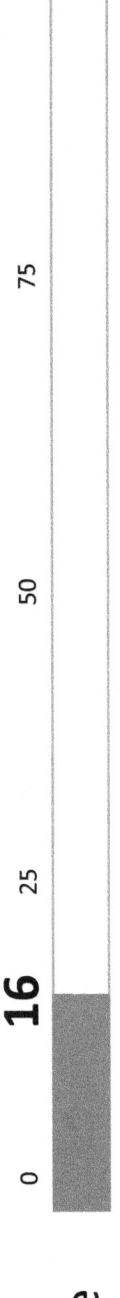

life expectancy in nature

weigh up to   14 kg (31 lb)

Banteng

The banteng is an ox similar in size and proportion to domestic cattle, but with a smaller head and more slender neck. Both male and female banteng have white rumps, stockings, ear tufts, muzzles, and spots above their eyes. The color of their horns ranges from bright white to brown with very dark tips.

life expectancy in nature

20

0   25   50   75   100

weigh up to   500 kg (1100 lb)

Flying fox

They got their name because of their fox-like faces and large, triangular ears. They mostly stick to a healthy fruit diet, which include sisal, cashew, pineapple, areca, breadfruit, jackfruit, neem, papaya, citrus, fig, mango, banana, avocado, guava, sugar cane, tamarind, grapes, eucalypt blossoms and more. There are 62 kinds of flying foxes.

life expectancy in nature

| 0 | **13** | 25 | 50 | 75 | 100 |

weigh up to   1,5 kg (3,3 lb)

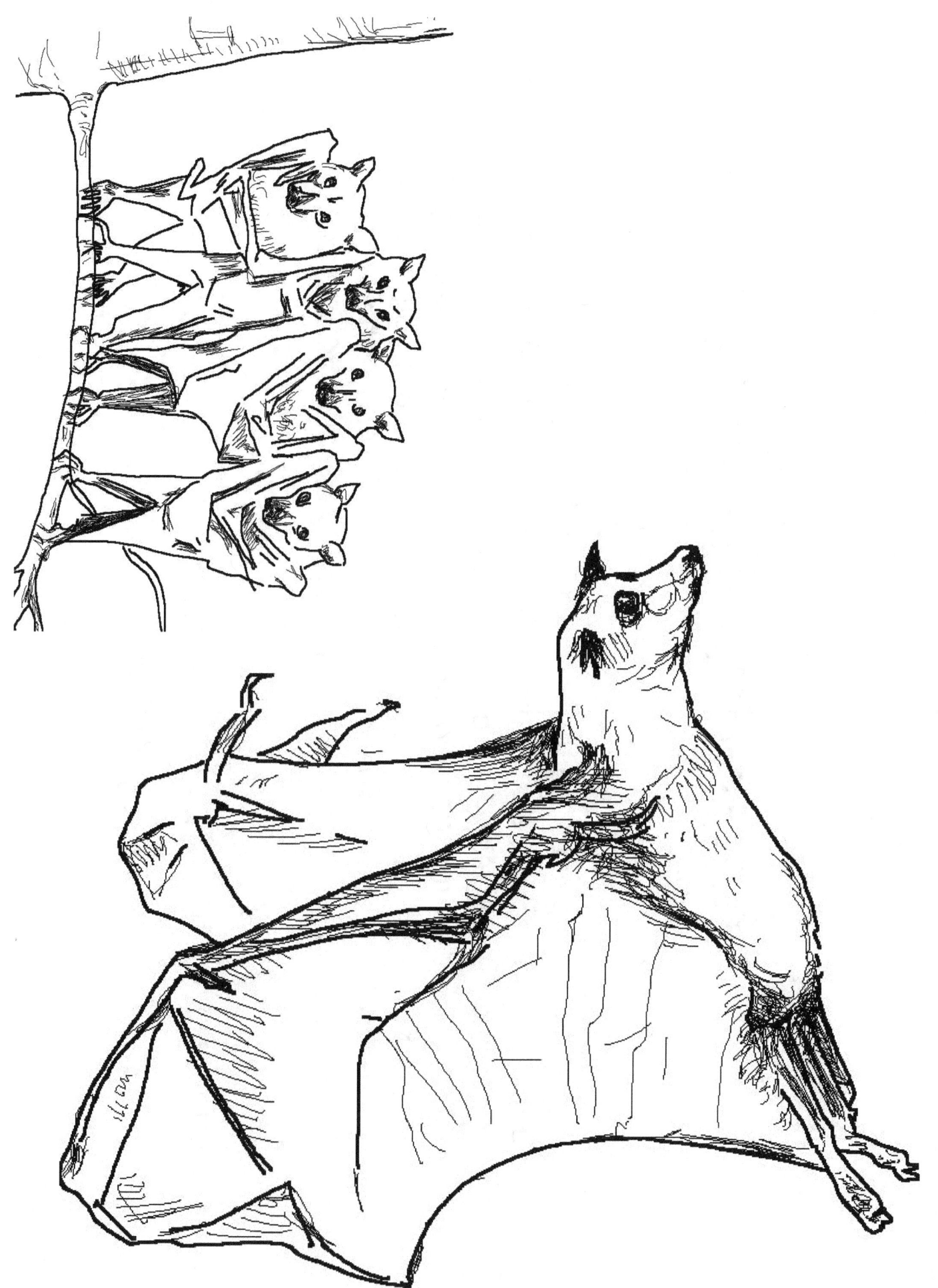

Monitor lizards

Most monitor species are terrestrial, but arboreal and semi aquatic monitors are also known. Monitor lizards differ from most other known species of lizards in that they have a high metabolism. This means they must be fed more often than other lizards. In fact, while they are referred to as "lizards," monitors are thought to be most closely related to snakes. They are considered rather intelligent and have even shown the ability to count as high as 6.

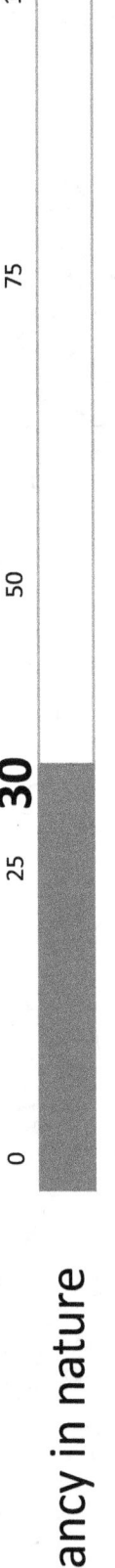

life expectancy in nature

weigh up to   60 kg (132 lb)

Bull shark

The name "bull shark" comes from the shark's stocky shape, broad, flat snout, and aggressive, unpredictable behavior. The bull shark has around 50 rows of teeth in its jaws, and each row has about 7 teeth, for a grand total of around 350 teeth in its mouth at any given time. The teeth are in rows that act like conveyor belts. When one tooth is lost, the tooth behind it moves forward, sometimes as quickly as within a day, to replace the lost one. They may lose and re-grow more than 20,000 teeth over the course of its lifetime!

life expectancy in nature

weigh up to   10 kg (22 lb)

The Southern Cassowary

This giant bird is found in Australia. The only bird heavier than the southern cassowary is the ostrich. Only ostriches and emus are taller than the southern cassowary. Cassowaries help spread seeds, which are returned to the forest undigested in the bird's droppings. The seeds of the Ryparosa tree have been found to be more likely to sprout after having passed through a cassowary!

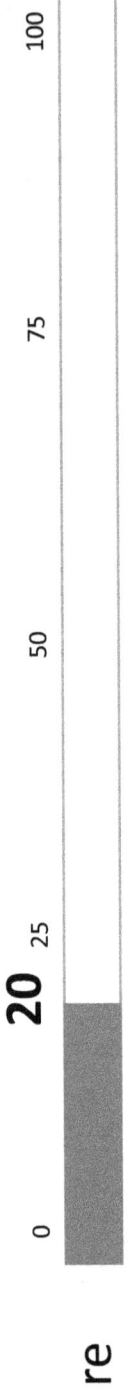

life expectancy in nature

weigh up to   80 kg (176 lb)

0   **20** 25   50   75   100

Cobra

Cobras are such domestic creatures! They are the only snakes that go to trouble of making nests for their eggs! They can eat other snakes, too. And only one animal is immune to its poison – a mongoose! What a lucky little guy!

life expectancy in nature

0   25   **30**   50   75   100

weigh up to   7 kg (15,5 lb)

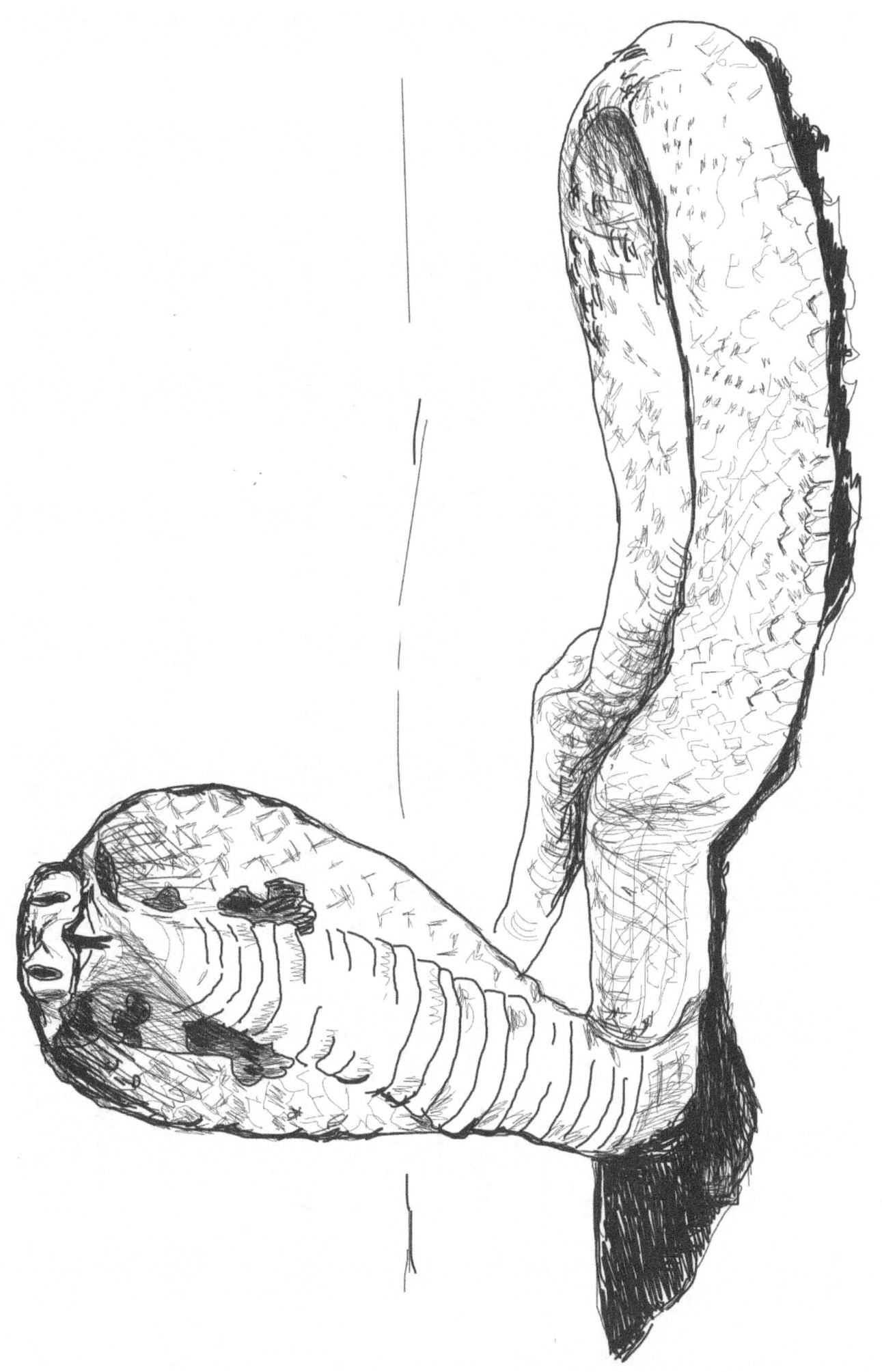

Hyena

Well, the ancient Egyptians got it all wrong when it came to keeping a farm. Instead of having cows and goats they domesticated hyenas and even ate them! Brrrr! Hyenas can solve problems in complete silence, using only non-verbal signals for communication! So, when you think nothing's happening, beware! These man-eaters are busy plotting....

life expectancy in nature

25

weigh up to   45 kg (99 lb)

Monkey

These happy creatures aren't just swinging on vines and eating delicious fruit! Some of them are trained and employed as harvesters of coconuts in Malaysia and Thailand! Wonder if the monkeys realize how much money they could have made had they been able to speak, too... it has been proved that monkeys can count, btw!

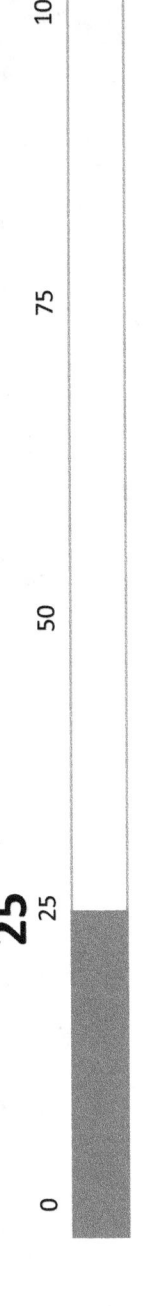

life expectancy in nature

25

weigh up to   8 kg (17 lb)

| 0 | 25 | 50 | 75 | 100 |

Vulture

Vultures are helpful every way you look. Having very keen eyesight, they can spot a carcass of a dead animal from four miles away! Why helpful? Well, they can digest meat which has been infected with bad diseases without any problem thus saving other animals and humans from getting infected! So, they are like 911 of the wild world when it comes to sanitizing the earth.

life expectancy in nature

22

0   25   50   75   100

weigh up to   65 kg (143 lb)

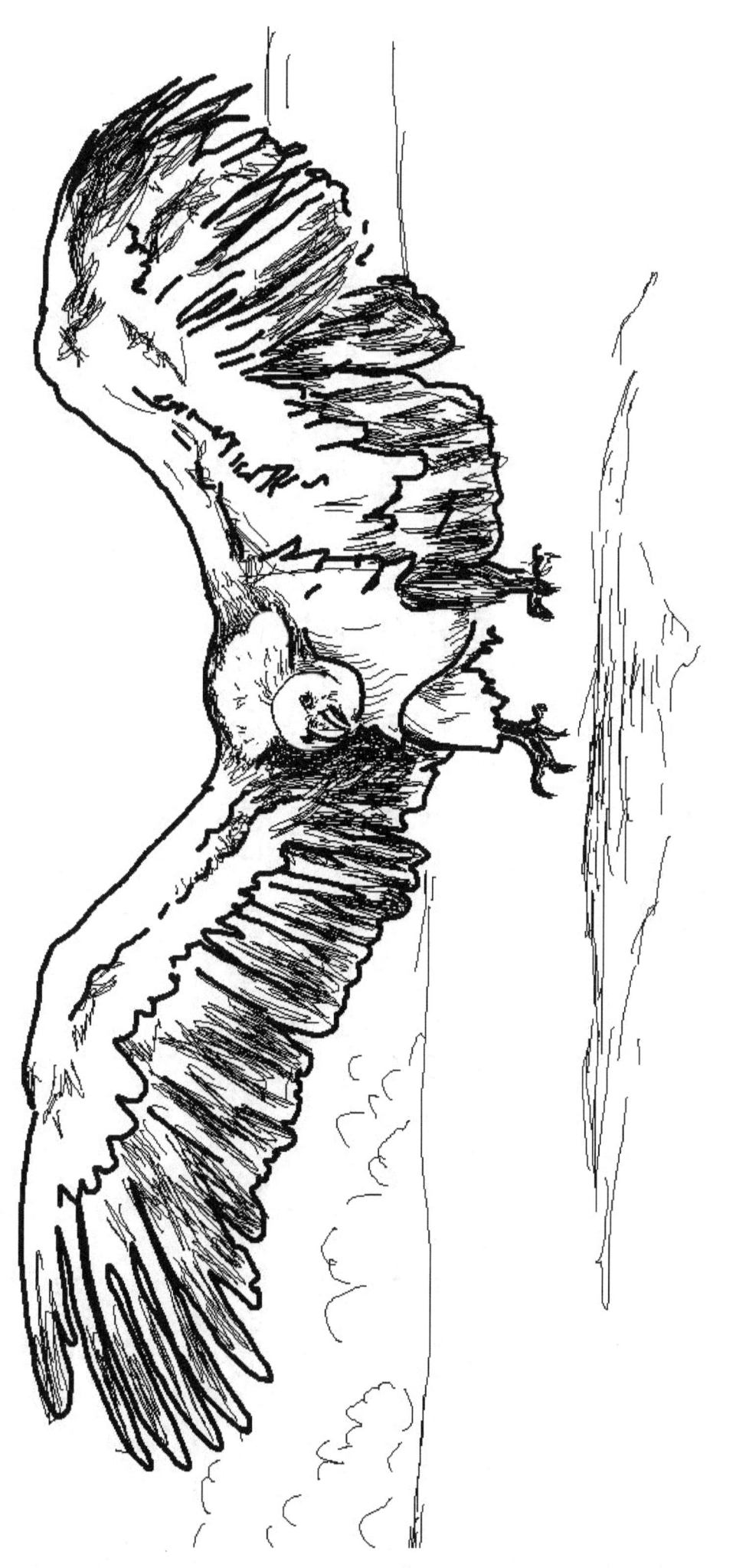

Ostrich

Ostriches have eyes that are bigger than their brains! In Africa people race each other on the backs of ostriches. And they don't bury their heads in the sand! When danger comes, they simply lie low on the ground and press their heads against the soil. The color of their feathers blends with the ground, so it may look like they bury their heads if you watch from a distance.

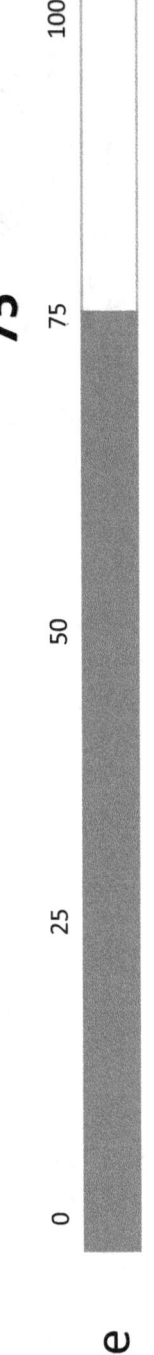

life expectancy in nature

0   25   50   75   **75**   100

weigh up to   160 kg (352 lb)

Flamingo

Flamingoes got its names from the Latin word 'flamma' meaning 'fire'. Their bright pink or coral coloration depends on a diet, since certain kinds of mollusks and algae contain such pigments. Nobody knows for sure why flamingoes sleep standing on one leg, probably, it's just convenient.

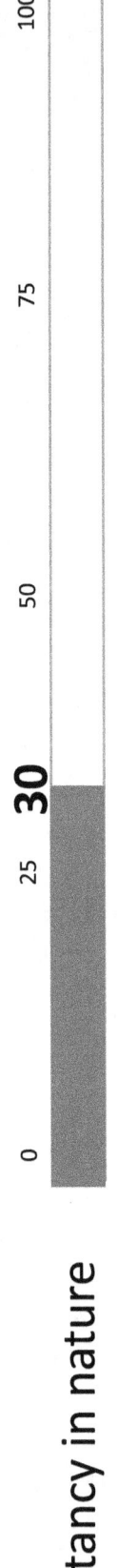

life expectancy in nature

weigh up to   4 kg (9 lb)

Marabou

Now, here comes the absolute champion in the nomination "The Creepiest of the Creepiest Creatures" – a Marabou stork! First things first. This bird poops on its own legs on purpose! You can't see its legs' true color – they are always covered with feces. Number two. This bird would eat anything. Dead, live, trash, human waste, you name it! On we go. You think they kinda look okay? Wait till it's their mating season! They inflate an 18-inch long balloon, called 'pouch', off the left nostril which dangles in front of their necks. They make a croaking sound through it and attract, well, their lifetime soulmates, which is very cute. Hold on, there's more. Their head looks like it's rotting but it's just the impression. When you dig all day long in some landfill or a carcass, you'd better keep your head bald and clean, so you don't get infected! Ready for more? They have a nickname which they got both from their looks and their activities – the Undertaker Bird. The black feathers of the back do look like the coats of those who prepare funerals. And while human undertakers take care of dead bodies, marabou eats them and thus prevents infections and diseases from spreading. So, there's a bright side for you. Whoof. And, finally, marabous are quite fearless. They would fly not away but towards grassfires to catch animals who are on the run from the danger. A nice plan to catch easy prey!

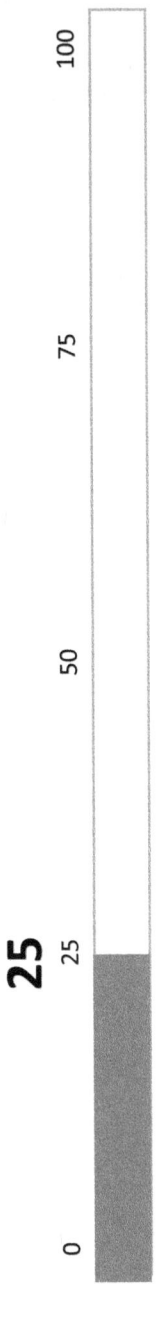

life expectancy in nature

25

0   25   50   75   100

weigh up to   6 kg (13 lb)

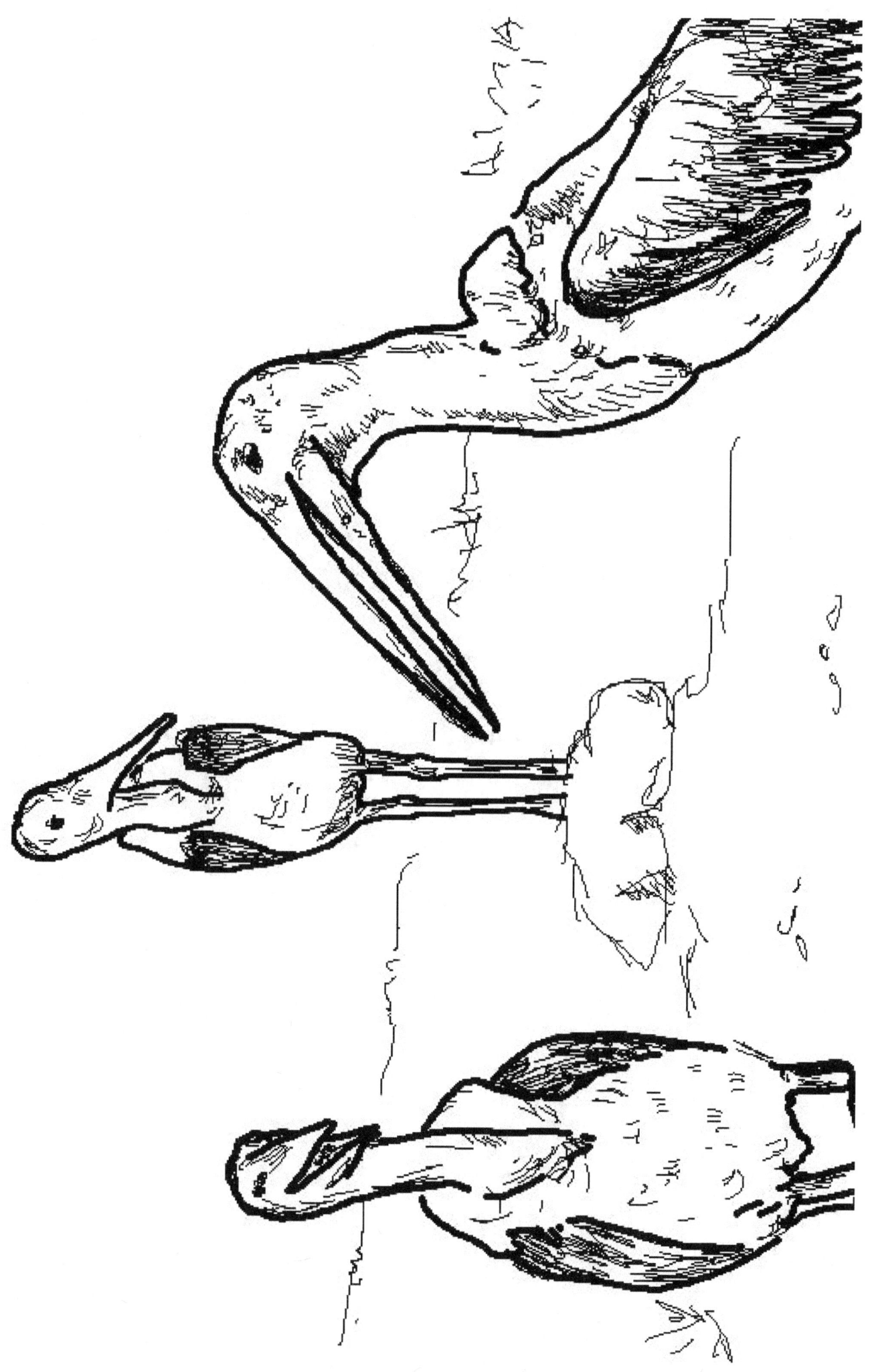

Dear Reader!

Thank you for choosing my book! Hope you enjoyed it!

If you really liked it, please, **leave a short review on Amazon!**
Use ISBN # 9781079224740 to find this book

Check out my website http://21centurywritersclub.com/ for more

books by me and my fellow writers!

See ya,

Mark

SEARCH MORE COLORING BOOKS

Book Series: Animal Planet

Animals of Europe

ISBN # 9781079222258

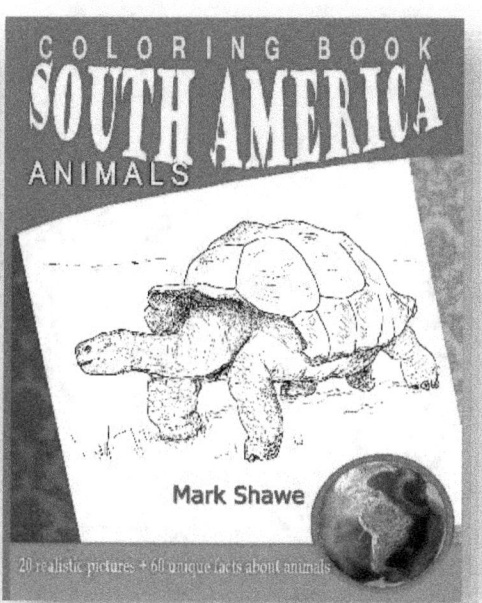

Animals of South America

ISBN # 9781079222920

Animals of Africa

ISBN # 9781079227536

Animals of North America

ISBN # 9781079225525

Animals of Antarctica

ISBN # 9781079225969

Animals of Australia

ISBN # 9781079226393

SPECIAL EDITION

COLORING BOOK:
ANIMALS OF THE WORLD

140 original realistic full-page images of wild animals of the World on single-sided sheets to prevent bleed-through

420 interesting unusual facts about the animals

BEST SELLER ★ No.1 ★ BEST SELLER

COLORING BOOK
ANIMALS OF THE WORLD
140 drawings

Mark Shawe

140 realistic pictures + 420 unique facts about animals

ISBN # 9781079226799

Book Series: **Animal Planet**